BASINGSTOKE
CANAL

Mark Hicks, a Basingstoke Canal employee from 1884 to 1966, pictured in the Chequers, near his canalside cottage at Chequers Bridge, Crookham.

BASINGSTOKE CANAL

DIETER JEBENS AND
ROGER CANSDALE

This book is dedicated to all the volunteer workers who helped to restore the Basingstoke Canal. We wish to thank the following for their help in selecting photographs and providing information: Kenneth J. Cattley, Liz and Tim Dodwell, Clive Durley, Tony Harmsworth, Janet Hedger, David Millett, Duncan Paine, David Robinson, David Gerry, Kim Threthewy, Dick and Alison Snell, and Philip Riley for his enthusiastic support and interest in the project.

First published 2007

Reprinted in 2008 by
The History Press
The Mill, Brimscombe Port,
Stroud, Gloucestershire, GL5 2QG
www.thehistorypress.co.uk

Reprinted 2010

© Dieter Jebens and Roger Cansdale, 2007

The right of Dieter Jebens and Roger Cansdale to be identified
as the Authors of this work has been asserted in accordance with
the Copyrights, Designs and Patents Act 1988.

British Library Cataloguing in Publication Data.
A catalogue record for this book is available from the British Library.

ISBN 978 0 7524 3103 1

Typesetting and origination by Tempus Publishing Limited.
Printed and bound in England.

Contents

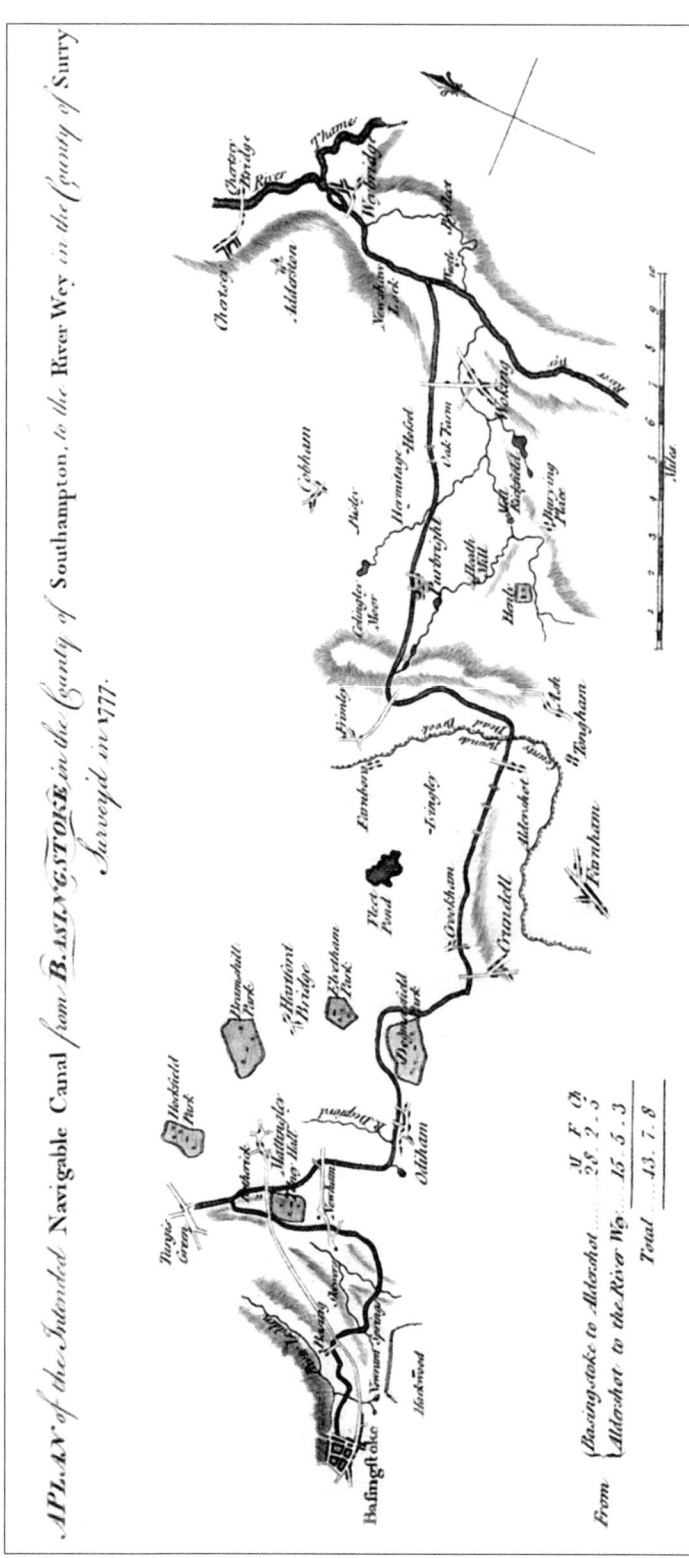

Map of the Basingstoke
Canal as originally
planned, published in *The
Gentlemen's Magazine* in
April 1778. The loop up to
Turgis Green was replaced
by the Greywell Tunnel
due to opposition from
local landowners.

Introduction

The Basingstoke Canal was conceived as an economical means of transportation for the development of agriculture in central Hampshire. The first route to be surveyed in 1769 was a line northwards to the Thames at Monkey Island, Bray, but the engineering problems proved it would be too costly. In 1776 a forty-four-mile route eastward from Basingstoke, to link with the River Wey Navigation and the Thames at Weybridge, was considered. The route included a loop round Greywell Hill that took the canal up to Rotherwick, with a short arm going to Turgis Green, but this met with opposition from the owner of nearby Tylney Hall. As a result, a decision was made to tunnel through Greywell Hill rather than go round it, and this route, reduced to thirty-seven miles, was approved by an Act of Parliament in 1778. However, work did not commence until nine years later, owing to financial restraint resulting from the costly War of American Independence.

Surveyed by William Jessop, the construction contract was awarded to John Pinkerton. From its junction with the River Wey Navigation at Byfleet, three miles from the Thames at Weybridge, the canal was built to rise 195ft via twenty-nine locks to Aldershot. The mile-long cutting at Deepcut, the 1,000-yard-long Ash Embankment crossing the Blackwater Valley on the Surrey/Hampshire border and Greywell Tunnel, 1,230 yards long, are the major engineering features. The canal was completed in 1794 at a cost of £154,463 – almost twice the estimated cost.

A Basingstoke Canal token paid to the navvies by John Pinkerton.

Timber, flour and chalk were the principal cargoes to London. Barges returned with coal and fertiliser. The canal did not prove to be a profitable venture; tonnages were below expectations, inflation led to rising costs, and road improvements from 1750 onwards made overland transport increasingly competitive.

There were plans to extend the canal to Portsmouth, Southampton and westward to Bristol via the Kennet & Avon Canal which opened in 1810. However, by 1866 no dividends had been paid to the shareholders and the original canal company was bankrupt, seventy-two years after the navigation was fully opened. The canal subsequently survived – if not thrived – on a succession of speculative owners.

None of the schemes for links to other waterways materialised, but local developments kept the canal in use. The construction of the London and Southampton Railway in the 1830s, followed by Aldershot Camp in 1854 and the short-lived brickworks at Up Nately in the 1890s, for which the canal was restored and deepened, all brought periodic trade. The last boat reached Basingstoke in 1910, bringing 10 tons of moulding sand from Mytchett for the local agricultural engineers, Wallis & Steevens.

Three years later, another attempt was made to reach the terminus in order to stave off a potential abandonment order under the terms of the 1888 Railway and Canal Traffic Act. A.J. Harmsworth, who then ran the only carrying business on the canal, set off from Ash Wharf on 16 November 1913 with a token cargo of 5 tons of sand. Over three weeks later the boat had only succeeded in reaching Old Basing. However, a High Court case between Woking Council and the canal's owners over the cost of bridge repairs decided that when the canal had first gone into liquidation in 1866, the liquidator had sold it without the benefit of an enabling Act of Parliament. As a consequence, the canal was judged to be private property and therefore not subject to the Railway and Canal Traffic Act, so the threat of forced abandonment paradoxically disappeared.

The most stable commercial period for the Basingstoke Canal was under the ownership of A.J. Harmsworth. He bought the canal for £5,000 in 1923 and secured contracts carrying coal and timber to Woking. However, his grandson, Tony, who himself became the canal manager in the 1990s, believed that his grandfather probably made more money from hiring out skiffs and punts and canoes than from his carrying business.

Decay

Alec Harmsworth died in 1947 and the canal was sold at auction two years later for £6,000 to a Purchase Committee convened by the newly formed Inland Waterways Association (IWA); the Committee's secretary was Mrs Joan Marshall. Legal problems appear to have arisen over raising the money to complete the purchase and Mr S.E. Cooke, a local businessman, agreed to put up the funds. Sidney Cooke formed the New Basingstoke Canal Company Ltd in 1950, and appointed Mrs Marshall as the canal's general manager. She ran it for the next fifteen years with the aid of about a dozen paid employees and a large number of volunteer bailiffs. The canal's only real source of income was a contract to supply water to the National Gas Turbine Establishment at Pyestock, but this ended in 1964. In spite of efforts to keep it navigable, insufficient maintenance, coupled with increasing vandalism, not least by the Army who blew up the gates of Lock 22, took their toll and by the mid-1960s the locks were decaying, the channel was silted up, choked by weed and rubbish, and much of the towpath had become overgrown.

Revival

The Surrey and Hampshire Canal Society was formed in 1966 to try and stop the rot. Unable to negotiate with the owner, who had his own plans for abandonment of the navigation, the society embarked on a seven-year campaign for public ownership and a policy of restoration. A successful outcome was signalled late in 1973 when Hampshire County Council acquired their fifteen-mile length. Surrey County Council followed suit by buying the Surrey length for £40,000 in March 1976.

By Order of A. J. Harmsworth, Ltd., and the Weybridge, Woking and Aldershot Canal Co., Ltd.

SURREY AND HAMPSHIRE

Byfleet, Woking, Pirbright, Frimley Green, Ash Vale, Aldershot, Fleet, Crookham, Odiham, Greywell and Old Basing.

PARTICULARS AND CONDITIONS OF SALE OF

The Old Inland Waterway

known as

THE BASINGSTOKE CANAL

running from the Wey Navigation at Byfleet to just above the Hampshire Village of Greywell, a distance of

ABOUT 32 MILES

together with the whole of

THE VALUABLE STANDING TIMBER

and the benefit of certain wayleaves and rents amounting to about per £345 - 0 - 0 annum

ALSO

VALUABLE RESIDENTIAL AND INDUSTRIAL PROPERTIES

adjoining the Canal and including

SPANTON'S TIMBER WHARF — WOKING

Let on lease to produce per £80 - 0 - 0 annum. Tenants paying rates

HOWFIELD COTTAGE — PIRBRIGHT

A detached country cottage let on a weekly tenancy to produce per £28 - 12 - 0 annum. Landlord paying outgoings

THE BOAT HOUSE CAFE — ALDERSHOT

Let on lease and producing per £65 - 0 - 0 annum. Tenant paying rates

Wharf House — Aldershot

Let on a weekly tenancy to produce per £39 - 0 - 0 annum. Landlord paying outgoings

LARGE BUILDERS WAREHOUSE AND STORE

adjoining the above and with the benefit of Vacant Possession

Canal Cottage — Crookham

a pleasing old world cottage, let on a service tenancy so that Vacant Possession could be obtained

LOCK COTTAGE — ALDERSHOT

a detached bungalow of which Vacant Possession could be obtained

THE WHARF HOUSE — ODIHAM

a pleasantly situated detached residence let to produce per £50 - 0 - 0 annum. Tenant paying rates

SEVERAL ENCLOSURES OF ALLOTMENT & GARDEN LANDS

BOAT HOUSES at Byfleet, Ash Vale and Fleet

ENCLOSURES OF STANDING TIMBER

All in hand at Fleet, Winchfield, Odiham, etc, which

MESSRS. ALFRED PEARSON & SON

are favoured with instructions to sell by Public Auction, in some 36 Lots, at

The Aldershot Institute, Station Road, Aldershot

on TUESDAY, MARCH 1st, 1949

Commencing at 3 p.m. sharp

(The only Lot for which offers will be considered prior to the Sale is Lot 1)

Illustrated Particulars and Conditions of Sale may be obtained, Price 4/- per copy, from

The Solicitors:
Messrs. Foster, Wells & Coggins,
Victoria Road, Aldershot.

The Auctioneers:
Clock House Farnborough Tel. 1 (two lines)
and at Fleet, Aldershot and Winchester.

50

Sale notice from 1949 advertising the availability for purchase of the 'Old Inland Waterway known as the Basingstoke Canal'.

Over the next seventeen years, the two county councils funded a programme of restoration actively supported by the Surrey and Hampshire Canal Society, the Inland Waterways Association and other canal restoration groups, who organised voluntary working parties along thirty-two miles of the waterway. The period generated a number of innovative practices, such as the operation of the steam-powered dredger *Perseverance* in Hampshire, manned by volunteers, narrow-gauge railway lines supplying work sites, summer voluntary work camps and youth employment training schemes. The protracted project was completed in 1990 and the canal was formally reopened on 10 May 1991 by HRH the Duke of Kent at Frimley Lodge Park, followed by a weekend of civic celebrations along the entire length of the canal.

Current Situation

The canal not only serves as a recreational amenity but is also a notable wildlife habitat. The alkaline water from the chalk springs at Greywell and the acid water content eastward, where the canal passes through heathland, has given rise to one of the largest varieties of aquatic plants and invertebrates in the United Kingdom. As many as twenty-five of Britain's thirty-nine species of dragonflies and damselflies inhabit the canal. Recognising the unique ecological importance of the canal, English Nature (now Natural England) designated the entire waterway, except for a length through Woking, as a Site of Special Scientific Interest (SSSI) in 1995.

Strategic management of the canal is provided by the Joint Management Committee, which has representatives from the two county council owners, the six riparian district councils, the Surrey and Hampshire Canal Society, Natural England and other conservation bodies. Day-to-day operational management is in the hands of the Basingstoke Canal Authority (BCA), based at the Canal Centre in Mytchett.

The BCA derives income from licences for boats, anglers and other enterprises, but the majority of its funding comes from the county and district councils. Most of the districts are not under a legal obligation to pay their contribution and some have not done so in full for some years, which has contributed to a considerable backlog of maintenance work. As a result of this and other factors, a review was undertaken in 2006 of the funding and management of the canal. Recommendations were presented to and accepted by the Joint Management Committee in the autumn of 2006. Perhaps the most significant recommendation was to abandon any further consideration of closing the canal to navigation, which at one stage seemed a distinct threat. Further study is to be done of various options, including the possibility of establishing a trust to run the canal.

Apart from lack of funding, the canal's other major problem is lack of water. It never had a summit pound reservoir and relied mainly on springs at Greywell to feed it. Increased levels of water abstraction, together with climate change, have meant that use of the locks has had to be suspended for large parts of the summer in most years since the reopening. This has obviously discouraged boaters from visiting the canal. The Canal Society has been promoting the idea of installing back-pumping schemes to enable the locks to keep working in dry periods.

The first of these schemes took water from below Lock No.1 and pumped it up a pipeline below the towpath to discharge into the Woking pound. The project was largely funded by the Heritage Lottery Fund and built by contractors, but volunteers also played a significant part. Volunteers did all the work installing a second scheme

Some of the boats at the Brookwood Rally in May 2006.

to back-pump the St John's flight, with funding mostly from the Canal Society and the IWA. A third scheme is being planned for the three Brookwood locks and possible reservoir sites are being studied to serve the Deepcut flight of locks.

It is certainly true to say that although the Basingstoke Canal has never been a very successful transport route, it has provided a highly valued recreational facility for the local population for well over a hundred years; in its heyday there were about a dozen boat stations on the top two pounds, where pleasure boats could be hired. However, the majority of the people using the canal have always been the walkers, cyclists, wildlife lovers and anglers who just enjoy its tranquillity. Their support perhaps has been the secret of its survival.

2006 saw the 40th anniversary of the Canal Society and the 60th anniversary of the IWA, so it was fitting that an IWA campaign rally was held at Brookwood to raise awareness of the continuing need for support for the canal. Over 200 boats attended the rally, which was a very successful event.

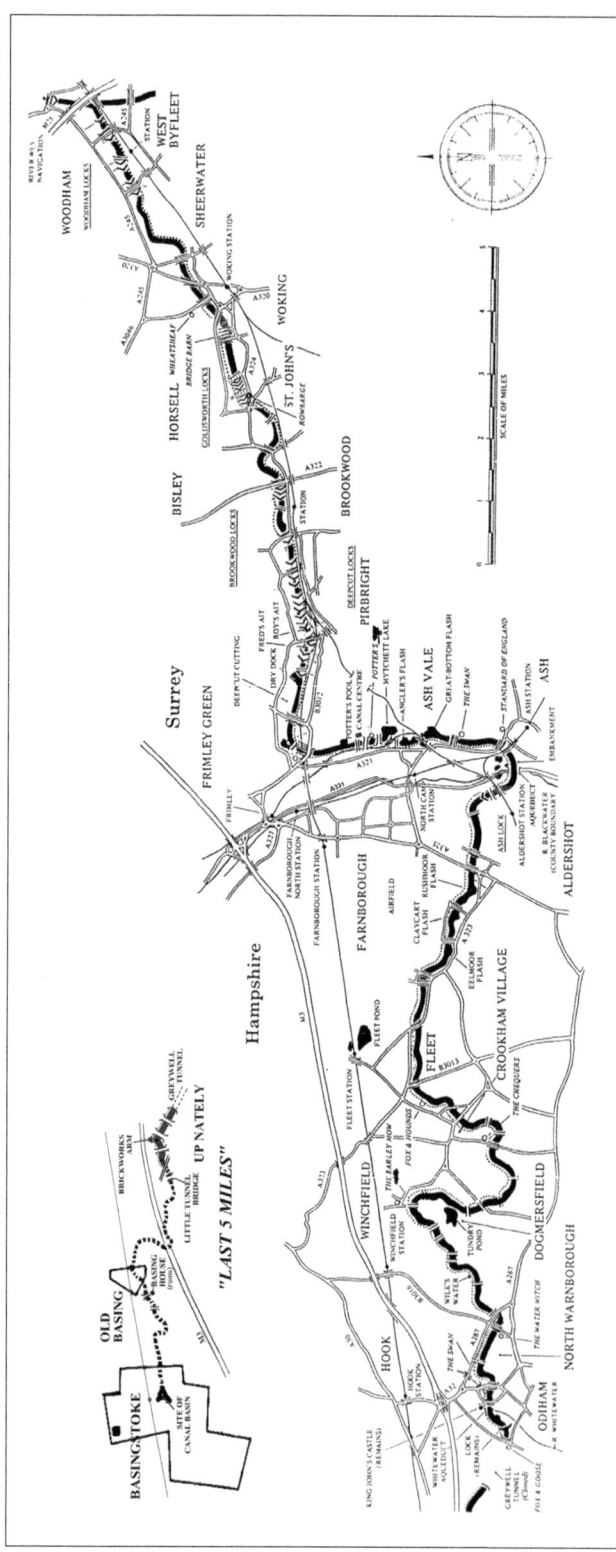

Map of the Basingstoke Canal as it is today. The limit of navigation is about half a mile east of the Greywell Tunnel. To the west of the tunnel, the canal is in water for about a mile. Beyond this point there are three intact bridges, the remains of others and the line of the canal can be traced round Old Basing, but there is nothing now to be seen in Basingstoke itself. The building of the M3 motorway when the canal was derelict, and the take-over of the damaged Greywell Tunnel by protected bats, have greatly reduced the chance of the last five-mile link to Basingstoke ever being reopened. However, the idea of a link to the Kennet & Avon Canal, first suggested nearly 200 years ago, has been raised again in a scheme involving a new canal joining the western end of the Basingstoke Canal to the Kennet & Avon, either at Theale or Reading. It would run parallel with the course of the River Whitewater, under the motorway and railway, and could include a new link back into Basingstoke. A footpath is also being planned following the old line as closely as possible from the western portal of Greywell Tunnel to Festival Place in Basingstoke town centre.

one

River Wey to Woking

The River Wey runs south from the junction with the River Thames at Weybridge and after about three miles arrives at the junction with the Basingstoke Canal. Immediately south of the canal, the London to Southampton railway line passes over the Wey. To the north of the canal, the M25 motorway also passes over the river and to complete the variety of transport in this area, aircraft from Heathrow Airport frequently fly overhead. A footbridge connects the towpaths of the Wey and the Basingstoke Canal.

The scene above shows a jubilant party aboard the Surrey and Hampshire Canal Society's passenger boat *John Pinkerton* as it arrives at the mouth of the canal on 11 May 1991, the day after the canal's official reopening. The boat left Frimley at 4.30 a.m. and after a long series of civic ceremonies and celebrations finally reached the River Wey in the late afternoon.

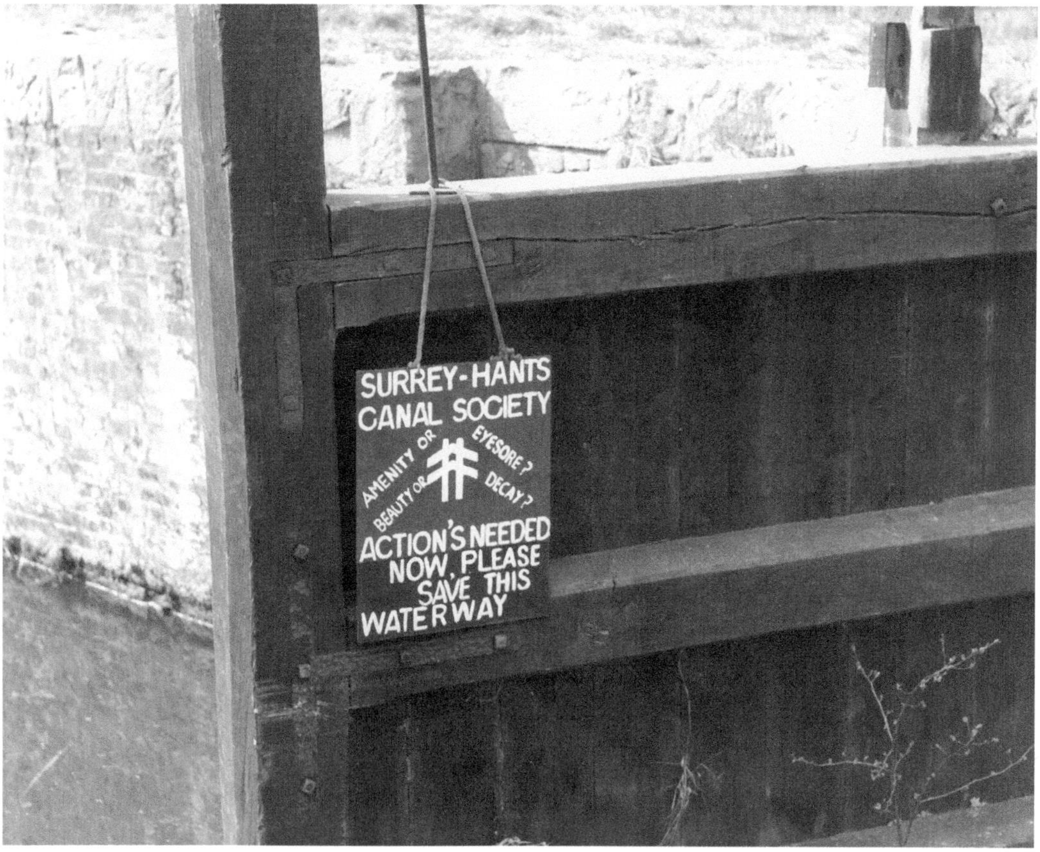

Above: Lock 1 filled with boats for the official reopening by Ken Goodwin, chairman of the Inland Waterways Association, on 18 September 1988. The lock chamber was restored by volunteers of the IWA's Guildford and Reading Branch, led by Dick Harper-White, at a cost of £1,200. 40,000 bricks were used.

Opposite above: Lock 1 in 1910, when cattle still grazed in the vicinity of the canal.

Opposite below: Easter 1968 saw the launch of the Surrey and Hampshire Canal Society's campaign to save the Basingstoke Canal. A flotilla of boats congregated at Lock 1 and this protest notice was hung on one of the bottom gates by Robert Harris, a founder member of the Canal Society.

Former working boats brought down from the Midlands in the early 1950s to be converted into houseboats. They were moored in various places above Lock 1, as far up as St John's.

A tranquil view of houseboats above Lock 1 in the 1970s.

Canal Society volunteer David Junkison pictured on a barrow run crossing Lock 5 in 1982. Restoration work was led by local resident and society member Pablo Haworth.

Canal staff, seen wearing the familiar tweed 'flat hats' worn by working men in the 1930s, fitting new upper gates at Woodham Lock 6, known as Sheerwater Lock.

Horse-drawn barge *Gwendoline*, built at Ash Vale in 1921, seen emerging from Lock 6 in 1934 loaded with coal for Woking Gasworks.

Narrowboat belonging to Beckett's of Kingston on the Woking pound in the 1930s. These were sometimes known as monkey boats.

Barge horse Charlie outside the stable attached to the lock cottage at Lock 3, in 1913.

A lady crossing over Lock 3 in 1904.

Lock 3 in 1986, with rotting gates and saplings growing in the brickwork.

Volunteers on a Waterway Recovery Group (WRG) summer work camp busily restoring Lock 3 in 1989.

A visiting narrowboat in the restored Lock 3, this was in 2001.

Sheerwater Bridge in 1904. Note the small boys on the towpath, transfixed by the camera.

Easter 1961. Boaters using a tarpaulin to sheet up the gates of the lock in an effort to make them watertight.

Popinjay in Sheerwater Lock in 1961. This appears to be one of the converted ship's lifeboats that were popular before narrowboats were built for pleasure use.

Harmsworth barge *Bluejacket* at Monument Bridge in 1913. It was built at Ash Vale in 1911.

Children fill the hold of *Glendower*, a former working barge, for a school trip from Monument Bridge, organised by Joan Marshall, the Canal's General Manager in the 1950s.

Boats moored beside the Boundary Road common below Monument Bridge, Woking, for a rally organised by the London and Home Counties branch of the Inland Waterways Association at Easter 1962.

Tim Dodwell at the helm of his cruiser *Firecrest II*, with his wife Liz and son Andrew above Monument Bridge during the celebrations marking the 150th anniversary of the completion of the London & South Western Railway to Woking in 1838.

Spanton's Wharf and timber yard in Woking in 1967.

Volunteers collecting shopping trolleys removed from the canal in Woking in 1988.

Trip boat *John Pinkerton* operating from the former site of Spanton's Wharf during the Woking 150 celebrations in July 1988.

A girl strolls towards Wheatsheaf Bridge, also known as Hospital Bridge, in Woking. This was in 1914.

The barge *Redjacket*, built at Ash Vale in 1909, unloading coal for Woking Gasworks, 1910. In 1940, *Redjacket* was sold and moved off the canal to the Lee Navigation to carry explosives from the factory at Waltham Abbey. The barge was destroyed in an air raid during the Blitz.

Anglers on the banks of the canal in Woking before the First World War.

A petition for public ownership and restoration of the canal, organised by the Surrey and Hampshire Canal Society in Woking in 1969.

Les Harris, a founder member of the Canal Society, at the helm of his cruiser *Santon*, while Geoff Sweet, standing on the bow, distributes leaflets to people at Step Bridge in Woking in 1969.

Rubbish removal by the crew of *Santon* at Arthur's Bridge in 1969.

A rally of boats at Woking in 1962 seen from Arthur's Bridge, with Brewster's timber yard in the background.

Annual Easter Rally of boats at the Bridge Barn pub in Woking, organised by the Canal Society and local boat clubs. The paddle-driven craft on the right is a weed cutter.

Dick and Alison Snell making and selling traditional rope fenders and crocheted shawls at the Bridge Barn Rally. Dick was a founder member of the Canal Society and their boat *Athai* is a familiar sight on the canal.

two

St John's & Brookwood

A flight of five locks takes the canal up from Woking to St John's and a further flight of three locks lifts it to the mile-long Brookwood pound.

Above: Maid Line holiday hire cruiser near St John's bottom lock in 1956.

Left: Langman's Bridge and Lock 7 in 1961.

Below: Summer work camp volunteers restoring St John's Lock 7 in 1985.

Mayor of Woking, Cllr Margaret Gammon, and Surrey County Cllr Michael Gammon with Peter and Margurite Redway, who led the restoration of the St John's flight, aboard the *John Pinkerton* for the official reopening of Lock 7 in April 1988.

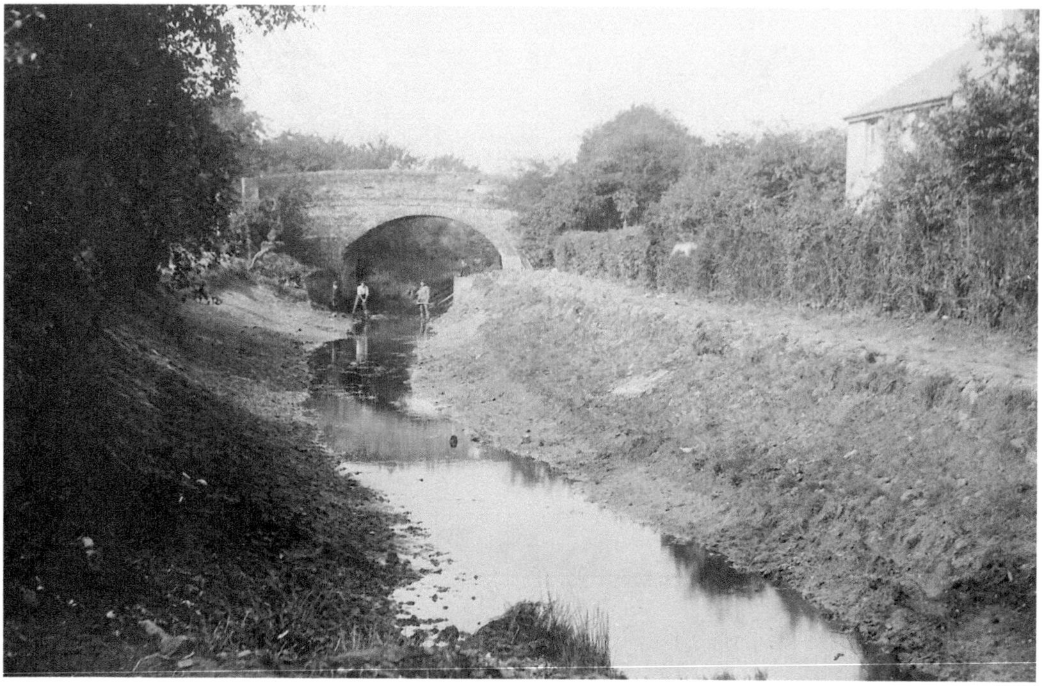

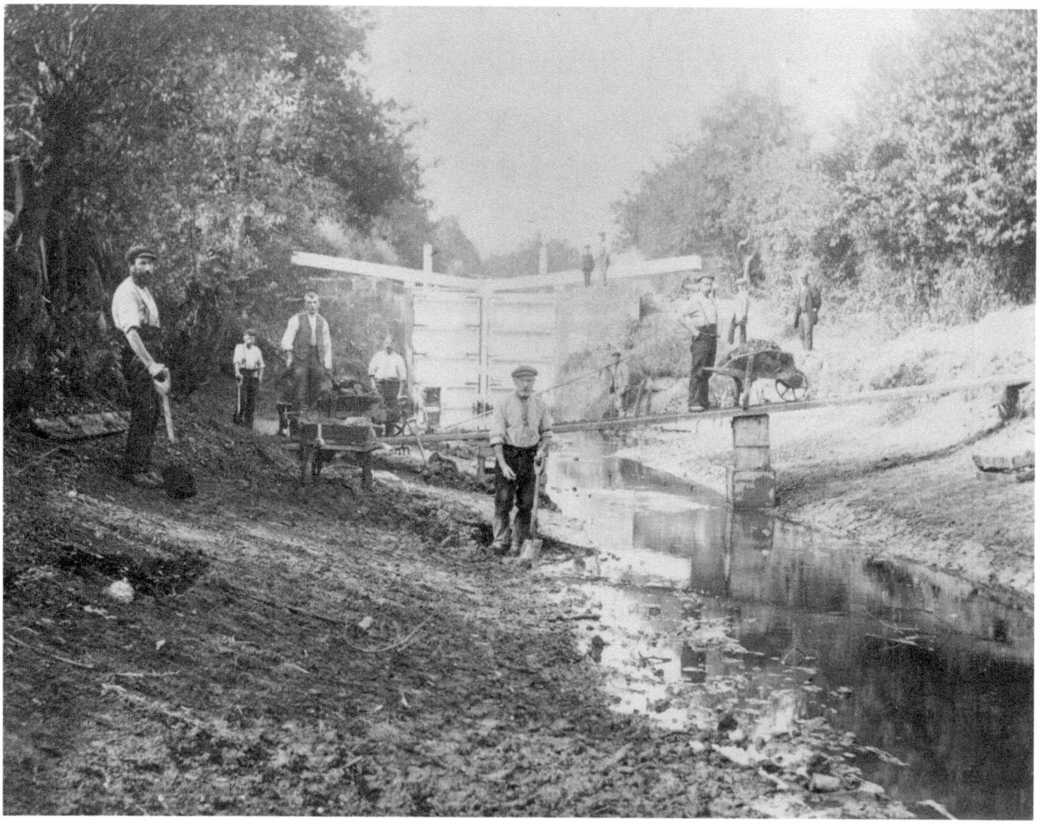

Above: Maintenance work below Lock 9, seen here from Woodend Bridge in 1913.

Right: A voluntary work party in 1983 demolishing decaying brickwork in preparation for renovating Woodend Bridge.

Opposite above: The canal drained below Woodend Bridge at St John's in 1913. Slocock's nursery is visible on the right.

Opposite below: Lock 9 in 1913. The gates were painted white after paint was accidentally spilt on them. The tools being used here are the same as those used to construct the canal 120 years previously.

Lock 9 and Woodend Bridge in 1988. Frank Jones (Job Creation team leader, centre) with supervisors Martin Smith and Jim Reid, who were full-time employees of the Canal Society for several years.

Lock 10 in 1913. The men were fitting new hollow posts. These form the watertight hinge about which the gates rotate.

Kiln Bridge, St John's in 1911.

An Easter cruise in 1958. Camping punts at Kiln Bridge.

Left: A voluntary work party rebuilding the chamber walls of Lock 11 at St John's in 1981. In the centre is Peter Redway, who later became the Canal Society's chairman. His wife, Margurite, initiated the restoration of the St John's locks by winning £5,000 in a national competition run by the SPAR grocery chain for the best local environmental improvement scheme.

Below: Frank Jones drawing the lower paddles of Lock 12 to let the *John Pinkerton* descend, the first boat to pass through since the lock was restored. This was in April 1988.

Lock 14: Cllr Mrs Pat Bohling, Mayor of Woking, officially reopened Lock 14 in May 1986. Robin Higgs, the Canal Society chairman, is standing on the far left.

Brookwood pound reopening in May 1986. Many local people came down to the canalside to witness the event.

Above: Brookwood pound after
reopening. This is Sheets Heath
Bridge in May 1986

Left: Mile Reach, Brookwood in 1915.

three

Deepcut Flight of Locks

The Deepcut flight of fourteen locks raises the canal by 95ft over a distance of about two miles. Its restoration was one of the greatest challenges to the reopening of the canal.

Rotting gates and saplings growing in the walls of Lock 15 in 1964.

Lock 15 was restored to working order in 1982.

Dredging by a Hymac excavator above Lock 15 in 1976. In the background can be seen the railway bridge, now demolished, that carried the branch line from Brookwood to Bisley Camp and the National Rifle Ranges; the train using this line was known as the 'Bisley Bullet'.

Deepcut Dig, a weekend working party held in October 1977, when an army of 600 volunteer navvies from all parts of the country converged on the Deepcut flight of locks to clear chambers, remove decaying lock gates and undertake other tasks in preparation for restoration. This is Lock 16.

Cruiser *Hailey* entering Lock 17, one of the first boats to ascend the restored flight.

Reopening of Cowshot Manor Bridge, Pirbright, in October 1982. *From left to right*: Frank Jones, Robin Higgs, Canal Society chairman, Paul Vine, author of *London's Lost Route to the Sea*, and Cllr Patrick Evelyn, the High Sheriff of Surrey.

Bricks being delivered to a Youth Training Scheme industriously working on Lock 24 in 1978.

Job Creation workers with their supervisors and project co-ordinator Frank Jones (centre), celebrating the completion of Lock 24.

The derelict Lock 25

Above: Derelict chamber and gates of Lock 25 in the 1970s.

Left: Lock 25 being restored by Canal Society volunteers led by Peter Jones.

Volunteers led by Peter Jones (centre) excavating a bywash channel beside the towpath railway supply line.

A canal breach above Lock 26, 1983. Part of the towpath was washed away when the canal overtopped the bank. No other damage was done and the breach was soon repaired.

Deepcut Railway above Lock 25, the brainchild of Canal Society member Stan Meller, seen here with his sons David and Andy, who both became civil engineers. The railway had previously been used at Odiham for transporting silt dredged out of the canal, and was later used to carry clay to line the Ash Embankment. The train on the right is on the main London to Southampton line.

A peaceful winter scene at Lock 27.

International Voluntary Service volunteers working on Lock 27.

Chris de Wet, founder and chairman of the Basingstoke Canal Boating Club, at the helm of his Wilderness boat, *Windrush*, below Lock 28.

The Lock Cottage at Lock 28 in about 1905.

The keeper of Lock 28 poses with his large family, c.1906.

Afternoon tea served in the cottage garden at Deepcut Top Lock 28 in the 1920s.

Lock keeper Bert York bringing a work punt loaded with canal reeds alongside his cottage garden at Lock 28 in the 1950s.

Canal Ranger Les Foster drawing a paddle to let a boat down Lock 28 in 1995. He started working for the New Basingstoke Canal Company in 1957 and retired from the canal in 1992.

Boats in Lock 28, August 1988. This was a special cruise to promote use of the Deepcut flight of locks four years after reopening.

Former Army swimming pool at Deepcut, converted into a lock gate building workshop.

A lock gate being taken to the adjacent canal to be floated down to the lock for fitting.

The derelict dry dock, infilled with dredgings from the Deepcut cutting, in 1983. It was rebuilt by the Youth Training Scheme recruits in 1984.

Canal Society passenger boat *John Pinkerton* having its first hull inspection in the restored dry dock in January 1985. The steel girders on which it is sitting previously formed part of a temporary bridge at Lock 17, which was rebuilt in the traditional brick design.

four

Top Surrey Pound

The top pound of the Surrey length of the canal runs from Lock 28 at the top of the Deepcut flight to Lock 29, having crossed county boundaries into Hampshire as it passes over the River Blackwater on a new aqueduct.

This pound in fact passes over two aqueducts. The first one at Frimley was built in 1838 to allow the London to Southampton railway line to pass under the canal. It was widened in 1902 when more tracks were added, and relined by British Rail contractors (pictured above) in 1981 in preparation for the canal's reopening.

A view across the canal from Frimley Wharf in 1911.

Frimley Green boathouse in the 1920s.

Replica Leeds and Liverpool Canal Company directors' launch, *Victoria M*, passing under King's Head Bridge at Frimley.

The Earl of Onslow, the Canal Society's president (left), HRH the Duke of Kent (right) and Robin Higgs, the society's chairman (centre) in the bow of the society's trip boat *John Pinkerton* on the occasion of the canal's official reopening at Frimley Lodge Park on 10 May 1991.

Above: L.A. 'Teddy' Edwards, an early and prominent member of the Inland Waterways Association, cutting a cake celebrating the reopening of the canal, with Jim Woolgar, instigator of the restoration (left), Paul Vine, author of *London's Lost Route to Basingstoke* (centre) and Robin Higgs, Canal Society chairman (right).

Left: Mrs Joan Marshall, former general manager of the canal, with her daughter Liz and son-in-law Tim Dodwell at the reopening of the canal. Tim and Liz were involved with the IWA rallies on the canal in the 1960s that helped to keep interest in its survival alive.

Opposite above: Sam Seymore and his son loading narrowboats *Mapledurwell* and *Basingstoke* with round timber (tree trunks) at Potter's Pool, Frimley, in 1916. The trees were transported to St Katherine's Dock in London for cutting into boards for the trenches in France during the First World War.

The remains of narrowboats *Mapledurwell* and *Greywell*, built at Uxbridge by the famous canal carrying company Fellows, Morton & Clayton, and the punt *Mudlark* in Greatbottom Flash in 1970. They were moved there in 1939 as anti-invasion obstacles.

Canal Ranger Peter Munt holding a handsome pike removed from the canal in 1989 by electro-fishing for the preservation of other species.

A training unit of the Royal Engineers rebuilding the canal bank at Mytchett Lake in 1978.

Ash Vale boathouse and, on the opposite side, the boat building yard can be seen in 1934.

Building the *Aldershot* in 1932. The barge was capable of carrying up to 80 tons and was ultimately bought in 1949 by Mr A.T. Harmsworth and renamed *Basingstoke*. It traded on the River Wey Navigation and the Thames until 1960.

Laying the bottom of the *Brookwood* at Ash Vale in 1933. The barge was ultimately converted to a houseboat and moored on the River Thames at Tilehurst.

Narrowboat *Basingstoke* after its return from the unsuccessful attempt to reach Basingstoke in 1913.

Ash Vale boathouse in the 1920s with a Canadian canoe drawn up in front. Punts and skiffs can also be seen available for hire.

'Uncle' Harmsworth, real name Frederick Thomas, also known as Ailey. He managed the boathouse at Ash Vale and had played for Newcastle United in his youth.

W.H. Harmsworth (left), who spent his working life on the canal when it was under the ownership of his father Alec, is seen here with his son Tony building one of a pair of gates for Ash Lock on behalf of the Canal Society. Following a career as a craftsman toolmaker, Tony became manager of the canal until his retirement in 2001.

Alec Harmsworth's canalside house at Ash Vale.

Ash Wharf, pictured in 1904.

A breach in the Ash Embankment in 1968. Following a long period of heavy rain, this oak tree blew over, taking the bank with it. This resulted in the draining of most of the top Surrey pound and the closure of the canal here until the 1980s.

WRENs from HMS *Dauntless* helping to reline the repaired Ash Embankment with clay, transported by the Canal Society's temporary railway in 1980.

Cllr Cecilia Gerrard DL, chairman of Surrey County Council, and Cllr Grahame Smith, chairman of Hampshire County Council, cutting the tape at the opening of the aqueduct over the new A331 road on 29 July 1995. Building the aqueduct caused the canal to be closed here for some nine months, isolating the Hampshire pound.

The boathouse below Ash Lock in 1910.

The *John Pinkerton* leading a flotilla across Ash Embankment during the Canal Society's second boat rally at Ash Lock in 1985.

Repairs at Ash Lock probably prior to the First World War. A temporary dam allows water to be removed by a pump that is belt driven by a traction engine.

The same operation, but from a different angle. Note the usual 'gongoozlers' on the bridge and the Harmsworth boat hire station – 'Boats, punts, canoes to let and built to order'.

five

Ash Lock to Fleet

Ash Lock is now the highest lock on the canal, with the rest of the Hampshire section originally, and now, all on the same level. At one time, a 30th lock, with a rise of about a foot, about a quarter of a mile east of Greywell Tunnel, eased the passage of boats to Basingstoke, but this is no longer in use.

An aerial view of Ash Lock Cottage (left) and Ash Lock.

Unloading flour at Ash Lock in 1916.

Preparing to remove the old gates from Ash Lock in 1980. Note the dam, then in place at the head of the lock, which was installed after the 1968 Ash Embankment breach.

Alec Harmsworth aboard the narrowboat *Basingstoke*, with a token load of 5 tons of sand, seen leaving Ash Lock bound for Basingstoke in November 1913 to demonstrate that the navigation was still in commercial use under the provisions of the Railway and Canal Traffic Act of 1888.

New lower gates for Ash Lock, provided by the Canal Society, being fitted in 1980.

Pictured in June, 2007, Ash Lock Cottage (centre) was built for the lock keeper in about 1810 and is typical of a labourer's homestead for the period. The cottage is a Grade II listed building originally with three rooms, the central one having a fireplace and three hooks in the chimney to hang joints of bacon for curing. There were three doors to the outside, one giving access to a privy. A bathroom, kitchen, vestibule and fuel store were added in 1954. The cottage was renovated by Hampshire County Council in the late 1970s. The crane seen by the waterside was acquired by the Surrey and Hampshire Canal Society in 1983 from a timber yard next to the Oxford Canal at Lower Heyford.

From left to right: Dieter Jebens, Canal Society Press Officer, Gwen Hubbold, a director of Johnson Wax of Frimley who donated £1,000 to the society to buy two Bantam tugs, appropriately named *Pledge* and *Sparkle*, Robin Higgs, Canal Society chairman, and working party leader Frank Jones. This photograph was taken in 1976.

HRH Queen Mary watching the Army rafting at Aldershot in 1913.

Queen's Avenue Bridge, Aldershot c.1910.

German prisoners of war unloading *Dauntless* in 1917. The canal was run by the Royal Engineers during the war and the last commercial loads to leave Aldershot were aeroplane spares from the Royal Aircraft Establishment (formerly Factory) at Farnborough, bound for Woolwich Arsenal in 1921.

Wharf Bridge at Aldershot. A message on the postcard from a First World War soldier notes that the Royal Engineers' yard was just to the left of the cottage. The Farnham Road Wharf itself was on the left in front of the bridge.

South Camp boathouse above Wharf Bridge in 1908.

Royal Engineers practising bridge building near Aldershot. The canal passes through extensive Army camps and exercise areas in the Aldershot area and was often used for training

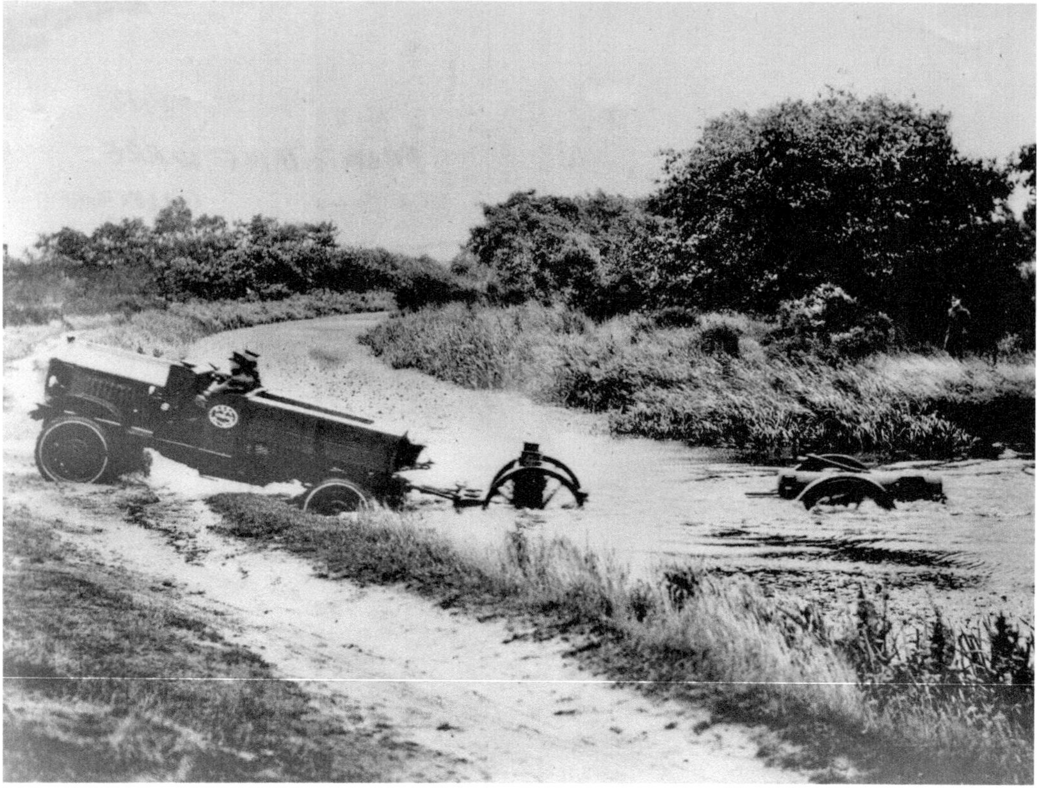

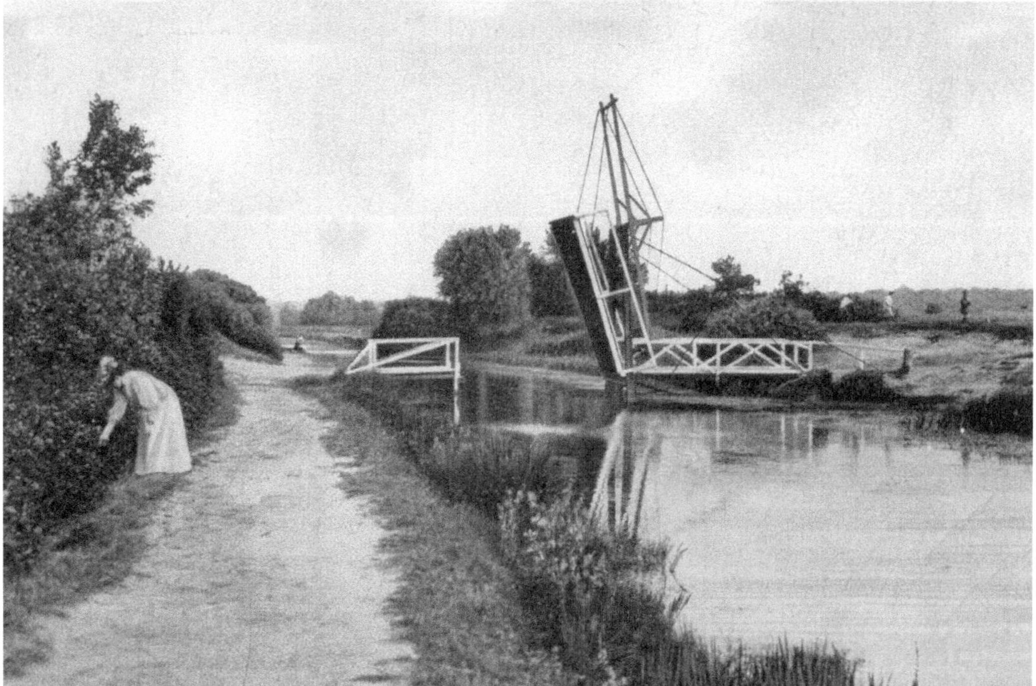

Right: Samuel Cody coming in over Eelmoor Flash to land on Laffan's Plain, Farnborough, where, on 16 October 1908, he had become the first person in Britain to make a powered flight, covering a distance of 1,390ft. In 1913 he and his passenger W.H.B. Evans, the Hampshire County Cricket captain, were killed when his aeroplane crashed at nearby Ball Hill.

Below: In the slipstream of Samuel Cody, a Russian Ilyushin Il-76 comes in over Eelmoor Flash to land at the Farnborough Air Show.

Opposite above: The Army on exercise at the canal during the First World War.

Opposite below: Military lift bridge at Claycart near Aldershot, 1909.

Opposite above: Norris Bridges, old and new, with the canal newly dredged by excavators during the summer of 1978. The disused old bridge collapsed a year later.

Opposite below: Span for a second Norris Bridge, to form a roundabout being put in place in 2001.

Left: The site of the canal breach between Eelmoor and Claycart Bridges that flooded Farnborough Airfield on the eve of the 1968 air show.

Following abortive night-long attempts by the Army to stem the breach with sandbags, the canal was dammed by the employees of the Royal Aircraft Establishment (RAE) and the hole in the bank was finally plugged with an old aircraft fuselage. The Canal Company subsequently sued the RAE for trespass and the RAE sued them for damages; the RAE won.

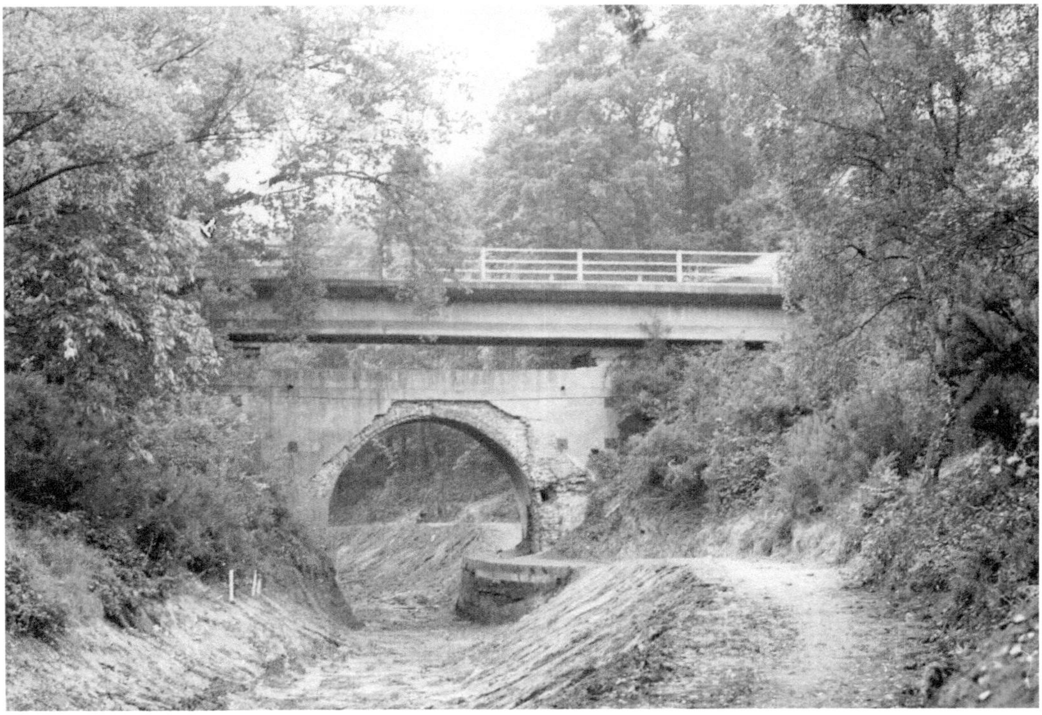

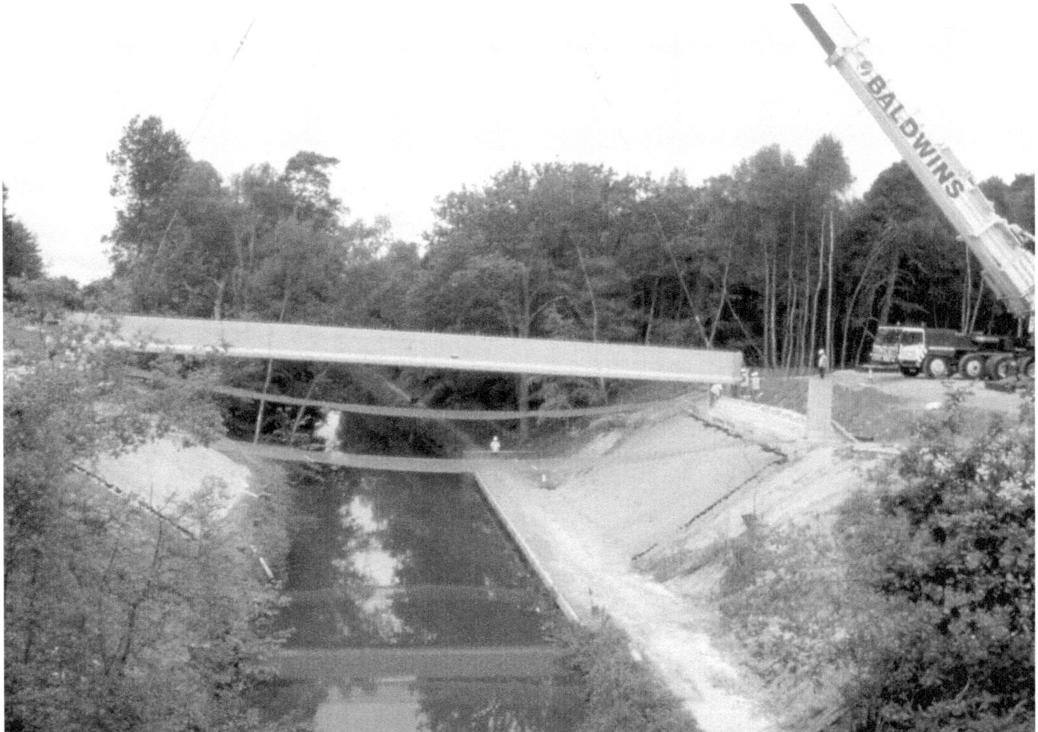
BALDWINS

The Forest Hut near Norris Bridge, a popular picnic spot in the 1920s. The National Gas Turbine Establishment, built at nearby Pyestock, took water from the canal near here during the 1950s and provided the Canal Company with its main source of income; the contract ended in 1964.

Pondtail Bridge, Fleet, in 1911.

Children playing on the ice at Reading Road Bridge, Fleet, possibly during the hard winter of 1947.

Summer at Reading Road Bridge, with children fishing for tiddlers. The bridge was lowered for the benefit of motorists during the late 1950s when the canal was disused. With two new bridges of similar height built at about the same time at Pondtail and Farnborough Road, it now presents an obstruction to the passage of taller boats. The maximum air draught is 1.78m.

A regatta near Reading Road in Fleet, probably before the First World War.

A canoe trial at Reading Road Bridge in 1979. Several members of the Basingstoke Canal Canoe Club have gone on to compete for their country, including Helen Reeves who won a Bronze Medal in the 2004 Olympics.

Fleet Carnival in 1956. Mrs Joan Marshall accompanies barge horse Kitty pulling the Canal Company float.

Canal Society float, *Hi-n-Dri* at Fleet Carnival in 1982.

Rowing at the Fox & Hounds pub, Fleet, *c.*1908.

Basingstoke Canal Boating Club rally at the Fox & Hounds in the 1990s. This friendly local event
normally takes place during the August Bank Holiday. The sloping bank behind the pub also provides
the venue for an annual performance by the touring Mikron Theatre Company.

six

Crookham to Broad Oak

After leaving the outskirts of Fleet, the canal enters its most rural and, arguably, most beautiful section. During the years of neglect, tree growth was largely uncontrolled and this length is now heavily wooded. Although this contributes to the canal's charm, it has other adverse effects. The trees take water from the canal, drop their leaves in the water, which turn to silt, and shade the aquatic plants from the light that they need. A programme of cutting the trees back is slowly having an effect and, when carefully done, the results are not unattractive.

Malthouse Bridge in Crookham, 1905.

Crookham swing bridge in 1907.

Children looking for coins at the Crookham swing bridge in 1937. Local children earned pocket money by opening the bridge for boats. Inevitably, coins sometimes fell into the canal, much to the children's dismay.

The *Basingstoke* passing under Poulter's Bridge in November 1913 during Alec Harmsworth's attempt to reach Basingstoke.

A final journey: Mark Hick's funeral procession passing under Poulter's Bridge at Crookham in 1966. In 1884, at the age of just ten, Mark had started working for the London and Hampshire Canal Company, the third owner of the Basingstoke Canal. He was still working on the canal four days before he died at the age of ninety-two, earning him a place in the Guinness Book of Records.

William Randall and his wife. He was the Crookham wharfinger until he retired in 1926.

Narrowboat *Tipton* in the winding hole at Chequers Bridge, Crookham, in the 1920s. Its remains were finally removed when the canal was dredged in the 1980s.

Basingstoke Canal Canoe Club Boxing Day's meeting at Chequers Wharf, Crookham, in 1987.

Chequers Bridge cottage. Mark Hicks and Captain, the barge horse, are pictured with an IWA boat trip in the foreground in 1962. Mark lived in the cottage, which included a stable for the barge horses.

Mark Hicks hiring out boats from his cottage at Chequers Bridge in 1966.

Chequers Bridge. This photograph was taken during the 1890s.

Coxmoor Bridge with Second World War anti-invasion defences. The arch of the bridge partially collapsed and was demolished in the winter of 1975/76. There was no money available to rebuild it at the time and there was no longer a real need for a bridge here.

Coxmoor swing bridge in around 1910. The bridge no longer exists although the brick abutments can still be seen.

Pilcot boat station at Chatter Alley, Dogmersfield, probably in the 1920s.

Gabion wall, which was built at Dogmersfield to support the canal bank after this began to slip when the canal was being dredged in 1982. The stone to fill the baskets was transported from the wharf at Barley Mow in the Canal Society's barges.

Barley Mow Bridge and canalside farmhouse, Winchfield, probably in the 1920s.

One of the Canal Society's barges being launched in 1983 at Barley Mow Bridge, where it had been repaired after being used to carry stone for the gabion wall. Tony Harmsworth, who became canal manager in the 1990s, used the technique that his grandfather Alec employed for the boats he built at Ash Vale. After props were knocked away, the boat slid sideways down well-greased skids into the water. Dogmersfield Infants School had been invited to spectate from the bridge.

Canal foreman Dave Gregory with barge horse Kitty and an outing of youngsters dressed in their Sunday best in the 1950s.

Inland Waterways Association canal trip with Mark Hicks at the tiller on 22 September 1957.

Sir Patrick Moore on the *John Pinkerton* in 1983, making a programme called 'Circular Motion' for an Open University series *Modelling with Mathematics*. He took the tiller under the watchful eye of skipper Clive Durley (seen holding the rail) to illustrate, with the co-operation of a cyclist on the towpath, how one planet passing another can give the effect of making the slower of the two appear to be moving in the opposite direction.

Stacey's Bridge, Winchfield, in the winter of 1906.

Opposite above: Sandy Hill Bridge, Winchfield, in the 1900s.

Left: A former Kennet & Avon dredger, *Perseverance*, originally built for the Grand Union Canal Carrying Company in 1934, was recommissioned and crewed by volunteer members of the Canal Society. It is seen here at work on the Dogmersfield reach.

Below: Dragline emptying a mud boat at one of the canalside silt dump sites. Although the mud was unsightly at first, it was very fertile and the sites rapidly became green again.

Pillar's Bridge, Winchfield. It collapsed in the 1920s and was not rebuilt.

Voluntary work party at Broad Oak Bridge near Odiham.

Broad Oak Bridge being rebuilt at a cost of £14,000, raised by the Canal Society. It was formally reopened in 1981 by the Earl of Malmesbury.

seven

Odiham to Greywell

When the canal was built it only served two towns, Basingstoke and Odiham. In the ensuing 200 years, Basingstoke has grown enormously but Odiham remains little changed. The winding hole at North Warnborough is the current limit of navigation, although small boats are occasionally allowed up the last half mile to enter Greywell Tunnel to check its condition.

Anglers and boaters enjoying the canal at Odiham, which is again a centre for boating with skiffs, punts, canoes and holiday boats available for hire from Galleon Marine at Colt Hill. The Canal Society's trip boat *John Pinkerton* also has its home base here.

Left: Mr Hall, the Odiham wharfinger in the early 1900s. Regular traffic to and from Odiham Wharf ceased in about 1901 when the Hampshire Brick & Tile Company at Up Nately went out of business. However, the occasional load of chalk to Woking continued to leave until 1904.

Below: The Great Wharf on the east side of Colt Hill Bridge in the early twentieth century. The house, which still exists, was then a pub called the Cricketers. The cricket ground was here on the north bank of the canal, until a new bypass road was built in 1981.

The Canal Society's dredger *Perseverance* was craned into the canal at Colt Hill on 29 July 1974. It had started its working life on the Grand Union Canal and then moved to the Kennet & Avon Canal.

A wedding reception on board the *John Pinkerton* in 1981 for John Brown and his bride Anna. Anna's father Stan Knight lived all his life in Crookham Village, as did his father and grandfather. As a parish councillor, Stan was a staunch supporter of the canal. He celebrated his sixtieth birthday by walking its entire thirty-two-mile length.

The Little Wharf on the west side of Colt Hill Bridge in about 1905.

Steam launch *Hero* at Nobsurd, during two days of waterborne activities on the canal at Colt Hill in July 1976. This was the first event organised by the Canal Society after the restoration began. 'What an absurd weekend that was!'

The late Graham Palmer, founder of the Waterway Recovery Group, the voluntary working party arm of the Inland Waterways Association, with Nobsurd Water Princess Julie Burke unveiling the new inn sign. The Water Witch was previously the New Inn, so named when it took over as the new local from the Cricketers.

The Water Princess living up to her title at Nobsurd.

Above: Tim Dodwell's yacht near Colt Hill, emulating the canal token sailing barge image.

Above: Dredger and temporary railway seen from Swan Bridge, North Warnborough.

Right: Installing the steam grab on the dredger. This replaced the ring grab, which just closed under its own weight, and enabled the machine to work much more efficiently.

Opposite below: Lodge Copse Bridge. This was originally a swing bridge, which fell into decay and was replaced by a simple plank, but eleven-year-old Louisa Nevill was drowned when she fell off this temporary structure in 1890. Although it was felt to be the duty of the Canal Company to repair bridges, the Hartley Wintney Rural Sanitary Authority was also censured for failing to ensure that this was done. The makeshift bridge seen here was made from old railway sleepers and rails and was replaced by a purpose-built steel bridge in 1998.

An early work party near Swan Bridge, North Warnborough.

Tony Harmsworth, David Robinson and Howard Diamond trying out a restored weed-cutting boat that originally belonged to the New Basingstoke Canal Company.

The swing bridge at North Warnborough in 1904. This was later replaced by a lift bridge.

John Pinkerton at North Warnborough lift bridge in 2004.

Left: A derelict narrowboat near North Warnborough swing bridge, pictured in *Country Life* magazine in 1903.

Opposite above: Boats at Odiham (King John's) Castle, which was built between 1207 and 1214. Legend has it that King John stayed here on his way to seal the Magna Carta at Runnymede.

Below: An aerial view of Odiham castle, canal and River Whitewater at North Warnborough. The canal runs up from the bottom of the picture with the river passing under it from left to right.

An unauthorised footbridge installed across the canal near Odiham Castle by a local land owner. This was removed when the canal was restored to allow boats to pass.

Dredger working above the River Whitewater. The original wooden culverts that allowed the river to pass under the canal were replaced by these concrete pipes when the canal was restored. They are visible here due to low water levels in the river.

Disused Lock 30, built about quarter of a mile east of Greywell Tunnel, three years after the canal opened. It aided the passage of boats through the tunnel by raising the water level by about a foot. The springs that are supposed to feed the canal are near here.

Narrowboat *Basingstoke* entering Greywell Tunnel in 1913, during the attempt to reach Basingstoke. Note the plank for the 'leggers' to lie on.

Canoes approaching the barred entrance to Greywell Tunnel in 1989.

Inside Greywell Tunnel in 1985. It is possible to go over half a mile into the tunnel from the eastern end before encountering a blockage. The tunnel was 1,230 yards long. Note the absence of a towpath.

The blockage in Greywell Tunnel, photographed in 1970s. A roof fall in the 1930s allowed clay to slip in and by the 1950s the tunnel was completely impassable. Any attempts at restoration are thwarted by legally protected bats that use the tunnel as a winter roost.

eight

Up Nately to Basingstoke

There is about a mile of recognisable canal to the west of the Greywell Tunnel, but the water stops at Greywell Road where Penney Bridge no longer exists. There are a few bridges still standing beyond this and the line of the canal can be seen round Old Basing, but all traces have been obliterated in Basingstoke itself. An attempt by Basingstoke and Deane Borough Council in the 1990s to reinstate the canal into Basingstoke as a focus for their new shopping centre failed to gain support from the Heritage Lottery Fund. However, there are plans to establish a footpath to link the centre of the town to the canal, following the old line as far as possible.

A dinghy next to the partially blocked western end of the Greywell Tunnel in 1970. A small group made an unofficial exploration of both ends of the tunnel.

The western portal of the Greywell Tunnel, believed to be in about 1920. A path to the left of the portal allowed the barge horses to be led over the hill to the other end, while the boats were legged through the tunnel. Two men lay head-to-head on a plank placed across the boat and walked along the tunnel walls, taking the boat with them.

The same view today. The stone side of the towpath to the left of the tunnel entrance is still there and the grill in the centre of the picture stops unauthorised entry to the tunnel. The portal has completely collapsed but the Canal Society has an ambition to see it rebuilt one day.

Eastrop Bridge, Up Nately. There were actually two Eastrop Bridges on the canal because the Parish of Eastrop was in two parts, separated by about four miles.

A Canal Society work party at Slade's Bridge, Up Nately, unloading tree cuttings for burning. Clearing the towpath has opened up a popular walk for local people. The far parapet of the bridge has been rebuilt but the near side is still to be done.

The bridge taking the towpath across the Brickworks Arm at Up Nately. Remains of a previous bridge found here suggest that it was raised in a horizontal position by means of ropes passing over pulleys at the top of posts either side of the canal to allow the passage of boats.

Left: The remains of a steam-powered narrowboat, *Seagull,* lie in the Brickworks Arm. It belonged to the Hampshire Brick and Tile Company and its construction suggests that it could have been built as early as 1850. It was uncovered by the Canal Society in 1984 and its engine was removed for display at the National Waterways Museum in Gloucester.

Opposite below: Even this remote part of the canal at Up Nately provided recreation in the 1920s.

Brick Kiln Bridge at Up Nately.

Opposite above: Harmsworth's attempt to reach Basingstoke paused near Penney Bridge in Up Nately. Stop planks appear to have been put in at the bridge, presumably to try to raise the water level in this pound.

Opposite below: Little Tunnel Bridge at Up Nately in 1991. The bridge is a listed structure, but the farmer on whose land it stands uses it as a barn to store hay.

Right: Narrowboats *Maudie* and *Ada* seen at Little Tunnel Bridge. They belonged to the Hampshire Brick & Tile Company.

Maudie and *Ada*, again seen at Little Tunnel Bridge, probably in about 1901.

The *Basingstoke* struggling with low water levels near Mapledurwell.

This is believed to be the swing bridge that used to take Frog Lane across the canal in Mapledurwell.

Moving one of the footbridges near Hatch to allow the *Basingstoke* through.

Journey's end – stuck in Old Basing, two miles short of its intended destination, Basingstoke. A month later, after rain, the boat was able to turn round and return to Ash Vale. Ironically, the threat of closure was lifted by a decision in a High Court case between Woking Council and the Canal Company over the cost of bridge repairs. The three judges ruled that the sale of the canal in 1874 had failed to transfer the rights and obligations of the original Canal Company. The canal therefore did not come under the provisions of the Railway and Canal Traffic Act.

Bridge in Milking Pen Lane, Old Basing, probably about 1900.

Basing House Bridge today, well preserved and acting as the entrance to Basing House but with no water under it.

The wall of Basing House with the canal in the foreground in about 1910. Basing House, at the time of the English Civil War, was regarded as the grandest private house in the country. However, the owners, the Paulet family, were Royalists and the house was totally destroyed by Oliver Cromwell in 1645. 800 gold guineas buried during the siege were reputedly unearthed by navvies digging the canal here.

Broadwater, Old Basing. This picture of what was clearly a famous local beauty spot was published in *Country Life* magazine in 1903.

Red, or Slaughter, Bridge, the last remaining bridge on the canal. Legend has it that a Second World War Jeep was buried under it when it was filled in.

Swing Bridge Cottages in Red Bridge Lane in 1905. The cottages are still there.

Eastrop Bridge in Basingstoke, *c*.1910. This was one of two Eastrop Bridges on the canal, the other being in Up Nately. It was demolished in 1927. The canal passed through what is now Eastrop Park.

E.C. White & Son, timber merchants at Basingstoke Wharf in 1900.

Wallis & Steevens, agricultural engineers, were based near the Basingstoke wharf. Supplies of moulding sand to make their iron castings were brought from Mytchett via the canal. This Wallis & Steevens traction engine, No.2,149 built in 1890, paid a return visit when it appeared at the Canal Festival of Transport held in 2000 at the Canal Centre in Mytchett.

Only one, poor quality, photograph is known to exist of the wharf and terminal basin at Basingstoke. This dates from 1904 and shows Eastrop Bridge in the distance and two of the boats that carried coal to the brickworks at Up Nately. The new Festival Place Shopping Centre now stands on this site.

Postscript

The Surrey and Hampshire Canal Society was formed in 1966 to campaign for the canal to be taken into public ownership and restored to full navigation. Following the canal's acquisition by the respective county councils in the early 1970s, the Canal Society formed a partnership with them to undertake the restoration. This involved the dredging of thirty-two miles of canal, the renovation of twenty-nine locks and the reconstruction of numerous bridges, weirs and culverts. Restoration of the canal from its junction with the River Wey at Byfleet to Greywell in Hampshire was completed in 1990 and the canal was formally reopened on 10 May 1991. Since then, the Canal Society has continued to work with the local authorities to preserve the canal and to improve its infrastructure. In particular, the Canal Society has been instrumental in providing enhanced water supplies through the construction of back-pumping schemes at the Woodham and St Johns locks. The society organises working parties, arranges canal events and operates a fifty-seat trip boat, the *John Pinkerton*, which is available for public trips and private charters.

Surrey and Hampshire Canal Society
Membership Secretary: Mrs Doreen Hornsey
Mallards
94a Aldershot Road
Fleet
Hampshire
GU51 3FT
Tel: 01252 623591
Website: www.basingstoke-canal.org.uk

John Pinkerton cruises. Tel: 01962 713564

The Basingstoke Canal Authority manages the canal and operates from the Canal Centre at Mytchett in Surrey. Visitor attractions at the Canal Centre include boat trips and a tea room. The BCA is responsible for maintaining the canal and issuing boat licences. Information about fishing, canoeing, boat hire and other canal activities may be obtained from the BCA or their website.

Basingstoke Canal Authority
The Canal Centre
Mytchett Place Road
Mytchett
Surrey GU16 6DD
Tel: 01252 370073
Website: www.basingstoke-canal.co.uk

The Canal Centre at Mytchett

Bibliography

Books:

Cumberlidge, J., *Inland Waterways of Great Britain* (Imray, 7th Edition, 1998)

Edwards, L.A., *Inland Waterways of Great Britain* (Imray, 6th Edition, 1985)

Gerry, D., *Towpath Walks by the Basingstoke Canal* (Surrey and Hampshire Canal Society, 3rd Edition, 1974)

Harmsworth, A., *Boats from the Basingstoke's Past* (Surrey and Hampshire Canal Society, 1969)

Horsfall, D.W., *Adelina* (Shepperton Swan, 1981)

Jebens, D., *Basingstoke Canal: The Case for Restoration* (Surrey and Hampshire Canal Society and Inland Waterways Association, 1968)

Jebens, D. & Robinson, D., *Basingstoke Canal Restoration* (Surrey and Hampshire Canal Society, 1985)

Vine, P.A.L., *London's Lost Route to Basingstoke* (1st Edition, David & Charles, 1968. Revised Edition, Alan Sutton Publishing Ltd, 1994)

Vine, P.A.L., *Hampshire Waterways* (Middleton Press, 1990)

Vine, P.A.L., *Surrey Waterways* (Middleton Press, 1987)

Note: Some of these are out of print but can be found on the Canal Society website at www.basingstoke-canal.org.uk/bkltarc.htm

Guides:

Cove-Smith, C., *The River Thames Book* (Imray, 4th Edition, 2006)

GEOprojects *Map of the Basingstoke Canal* (1995)

Jebens, D., *Guide to the Basingstoke Canal.* (Basingstoke Canal Authority and Surrey and Hampshire Canal Society, 2nd Edition, 2004)

Guide to the Waterways 7, Thames, Wey, Kennet & Avon (Nicholson, 2000)